THE WISE TURTLE:
AN ANTHOLOGY OF
SEVENTH GRADE POETRY

By ST PIUS X SCHOOL 7th GRADE STUDENTS

Copyright © 2016 by Dinsmore Homestead Foundation

All rights reserved

The Wise Turtle: An Anthology of Seventh Grade Poetry

ISBN: 978-0-9887117-6-1

Contributors: St Pius X School 7th Grade Students

Cover artwork by: Ryan Bosch, Claire Dunham & Paige Neuhaus
Back cover photo credits: Dinsmore Homestead Foundation & Brianne Donelan

ALL RIGHTS RESERVED. No part of this book may be reproduced or transmitted in any form or by any means, electronic or mechanical, including photocopying, recording or by any information storage and retrieval system without the written permission from the author, except for the inclusion of brief quotations in a review.

Published by:

The Merlot Group, LLC: 613 Main Street, Covington KY 41011
(859) 743-1003

Dedication

To the wise turtles of our lives—our parents and other family members, our friends, and our teachers

THE WISE TURTLE

Table of Contents

The Wise Turtle Poetry Project:

    Origins of *The Wise Turtle*

    "The Wise Turtle" by Paige Neuhaus

Why the Dinsmore Homestead:

    Background by Jan Garbett

    Students Reflect on the Dinsmore Homestead

Selections from *Verses and Sonnets* by Julia Dinsmore	1
Chapter One: Tributes to Dr. King	7
Chapter Two: Just for Fun	49
Chapter Three: Life and Faith	59
Chapter Four: Homeroom 701	75
Chapter Five: Homeroom 702	101
Chapter Six: Homeroom 703	125

Acknowledgments:

We thank God for our many blessings and recognize His hand in all things. With God, nothing is impossible.

We thank the Dinsmore Homestead for welcoming us during our tour of the house and grounds and for teaching us about the Dinsmore family and the history that lives on there. We were inspired by Julia's poetry, and we hope that her inspiration touches others.

We offer a major shout-out to Shawn Masters of The Merlot Group for his patient and flexible approach to our project and for sharing his expertise and wisdom as he traveled with us along our path to completion.

We acknowledge the work of all sixty-eight classmates in our seventh grade who worked on the book and donated their poems as Christian service to the Dinsmore Homestead. Way to go, seventh grade!

We cannot forget our sponsors who helped us to finance the publication of our book. We feared that we might overlook someone who contributed to our project after our book went to press, so we have attached a separate page of acknowledgment to each book so that we could include all sponsors, up to the last minute.

We thank our parents who supported our project and who continually encourage us in our academic efforts.

We gratefully acknowledge the faculty and staff of St. Pius X School, especially Mrs. Lonnemann and Mrs. Greenwell, and Father Baiju and Father Andrew of St. Pius X Church.

We thank Paige Brunson of Notre Dame Academy who assisted weekly in our classroom. She worked with us each Tuesday and helped us with our poetry project. Additionally, Rose Salmons for typing our manuscript.

We thank Mrs. Garbett, our seventh grade language arts teacher, who has helped us in many ways, both great and small.

THE WISE TURTLE:
AN ANTHOLOGY OF SEVENTH GRADE POETRY

November 5, 2015

Hiking in the Dinsmore Woods

One of our adult leaders trudged along, slowly, surely, walking stick in hand. I turned to Jackson and said, "Wise Turtle". He nodded in agreement. The phrase remained with us. It led us to a path of service. We did not turn back. It is true that we take chances in our lives, but in the end, what we achieve is worth the risk.

Ross Lux

The Wise Turtle

By Paige Neuhaus

As the blaze of the orange sky
    warms the forest,
  the wise turtle walks~
    slow and steady,
     walking stick in hand.
His thoughts are filled
    with colorful ponds
      and distant bird songs.

                        For the wise turtle,
                          it is not easy
                        to speak of emotions
                        that break the soul
                          and find a place
                          deep in the heart.

He trails his way home—
A long, hollow log—
    to sit and listen
    to the voices
    of the forest.

                        He hears sounds of joy
                          and love—
                          Birds singing,
                          and new life
                          in the world.

He hears the sounds of mourning—
    wolf cries,
    hawk calls,
    sad songs
    of the dove.

                    All-knowing, the wise turtle knows
                        that everything happens
                          for a reason,
                        And you take chances,
                    even if they change your life,
                        because in the end,
                          It is all worth it.

Why The Dinsmore Homestead?

It was an outstanding day in November, a cloudy but warm Indian summer morning when our seventh grade class from St. Pius X School visited the Dinsmore Homestead in Boone County. The students participated in old-fashioned games, toured the home, investigated the outbuildings (including the four-seater privy), and hiked to the family graveyard. They experienced a taste of what life was like for James and Martha Dinsmore and their family in the nineteenth century. They also learned that Julia Dinsmore, who ran the farm for many years, was a published poet. She not only farmed and mothered her two nieces, she also kept a journal for fifty-four years and published a volume of poetry, *Verses and Sonnets* (President Theodore Roosevelt was one of her fans).

After our field trip, I shared with the class that the Dinsmore Homestead was struggling financially. It is challenging to keep up with a one hundred seventy-four year old home with its surrounding grounds and farm buildings. The students decided that, like Julia Stockton Dinsmore, they too would publish a volume of poetry and honor Julia's name with their work. They would perform a priceless act of Christian service: All proceeds from their proposed book would benefit the homestead now and for years to come. In the language of the students: *We want to help the Dinsmore Homestead because it is such a wonderful place with almost two hundred years of history. The homestead needs to stay open, especially for students like us who want to visit it again and again. We want to see what will happen at Dinsmore for years to come—to witness what the next generation after us will learn and do there.*

The Dinsmore Homestead is a rare treasure in the midst of rapid growth and development in Northern Kentucky. An essential part of its mission is to provide educational opportunities for life-long learners of all ages. Like many other nonprofit sites, it struggles every year to remain open. Its history reaches back in time to President George Washington who was a friend of two members of the extended family—Silas Dinsmoor and Alexander Macomb. James' granddaughter, Patty Selmes, was a neighbor of Theodore Roosevelt when both owned ranches in the Dakota Territory. Patty's daughter, Isabella, remained a close friend of Eleanor Roosevelt throughout her life. And it is impossible to ignore the presence of the African American history that resides there in the remembrance of people, both enslaved and free, whose strength and talents both built and sustained the homestead. In short, Dinsmore is a microcosm of regional, state, national, and global history.

My second grade class from Kelly Elementary was one of the first to visit Dinsmore in 1989. Martha Breasted, the great-great granddaughter of James and Martha, was living there part-time (her main residence was in Arizona). As my class viewed the home and artifacts with awe and wonder, Martha, with her crown of white hair, peeked around the corner to spy on the children. She loved to see the students visit; she found great joy in sharing her home and family stories with eager learners.

Now it is the year 2016. Many groups of students have come and gone from Dinsmore. My second graders from 1989 have their own families. Their children no doubt have experienced a Dinsmore field trip. As the seventh graders of St. Pius have said, the Dinsmore Homestead must continue on "for years to come". It is our fervent prayer that *The Wise Turtle: An Anthology of Seventh Grade Poetry,* will aid that cause and honor the Dinsmore name for generations to come.

                Jannes Garbett, teacher
                St. Pius X School

Students Reflect on the Dinsmore Homestead

When I saw the bathtubs in the bedrooms, it made me appreciate how well-preserved the house is.

Isabelle Bennett

I had the role of Patty Selmes, and I learned that she was a very pretty redhead. Her only child was Isabella who was also very pretty. [Isabella Selmes Ferguson Greenway King was the mother of Martha Ferguson Breasted who turned over her home to the Dinsmore Homestead Foundation.]

Ava Quigley

The portrait of James Dinsmore in the parlor tells me that the family had respect for him. It was the nicest room in the house so it is obviously an important picture. It seemed like James' eyes followed me around the room.

Jason Reid

The homestead is very old;

It might be growing mold.

It was a very fun place to be;

I wanted to stay and have tea.

Olivia Maschinot

My favorite artifact was the bird nest containing the hair of one of Julia's nieces [Patty]. It brings the home to reality because a part of her is still in the house.

Annabelle Sunday

We saw an old hat rack. It tells me that the Dinsmore family loved visitors. I am interested in this because of all the hats belonged to different people [who had visited there].

Ethan Wever

The picture signed by Theodore Roosevelt told me that the Dinsmores had a very close connection with the Roosevelts. This artifact is interesting to me because it is extremely old and Roosevelt was a popular President. This [the picture] is special because it was autographed by President Roosevelt, and I have never seen an actual presidential autograph before.

Trey Gronotte

> Oh, the graveyard is dark,
> But the house is so great.
> The games are much fun,
> Although there is absolutely
> No chewing gum!

Anonymous

One artifact I observed was the baby grand piano. It told me that the Dinsmore family was very artistic.

Jaden Siemer

I was fascinated by the ice house. It shows how hard the enslaved people worked. It is interesting to me because they cut the ice from the river which is about a mile from the Dinsmore Homestead.

Claire Edgington

I learned that Susan Bell Dinsmore was the youngest of the Dinsmore sisters and that she died very young in a boating accident. I picture her being a bubbly, fun, and kind girl, someone very generous.

Jenna Danneman

The many books showed me that the family members were well-educated. I was especially interested in the encyclopedias and the giant dictionary.

Ross Lux

I took on the role of Sally, a slave. She had seven children. I think that life would be hard for her because she probably worked long hours even with having a lot of kids to care for.

Skyllar Jacocks

I took the role of Martha Dinsmore, wife of James Dinsmore. In my role as Martha, I had three children: Isabella, Julia, and Susan. I picture Martha ringing the bell when it was time to eat, and sitting down reading a book, and talking with her daughters.

Abby Powers

As Isabella Dinsmore Flandrau, my wedding to Charles Flandrau was held in the parlor. That room was used for parties or even for funerals.

Kierstin Haas

I was Isabella Selmes Ferguson Greenway King, the first Congresswoman from Arizona. She was very smart and beautiful.

Corinne Laws

Eugenia Wadsworth was the teacher who taught the Dinsmore girls in their home. She probably earned a little bit of money for her work, unlike the slaves.

Lauren Davey

Martha Ferguson Breasted turned the Dinsmore Homestead into an open house museum, especially so that children could learn about life in the past.

Grace Martin

The identity I assumed was James Dinsmore. I learned that he, along with his brother and some slaves, built the entire house. It took three years. I picture his life in Boone County as being relaxed. He probably told his slaves what to do in the morning, did a little work himself, and then relaxed.

Collin Gerwe

I learned that Silas Dinsmoor was the first person to be buried in the family graveyard. He knew George Washington and showed James, his nephew, the land where the Dinsmore house stands today. He would not have lived on the farm, only visited.

Drew Kent

I learned that James Dinsmore founded the Dinsmore home. Even though as a child he hated the thought of owning slaves, he later accepted the idea. James' daily life was likely spent reading and sitting at the table.

Chris Mason

The identity I assumed was Martha Macomb Dinsmore, wife of James. She was the mother of three girls. Her funeral was held in the parlor. I imagine her as a lovely wife, mother, and person.

Ella Weaver

Selection of Poems from

Verses and Sonnets composed by

Miss Julia Dinsmore

Reprinted with permission from the Dinsmore Homestead Foundation

THE CLOCK'S REPLY

A little girl sat in the door of a hall,
And heard the faint clock crooning there
The monotonous message Time sends to all,
And said with a willful, petulant air,
"Hurry, old clock, you are so slow,
I'm tired of hearing you tick and tick;
You are always starting and back you go,
I want you to change and whirl round quick.
I'm tired and sick of being small,
And having to mind and study too;
I want to be free and wise and tall-
Tall and minded, old clock, like you.
My nest is empty, my birds have flown,-
I saw it just now tho' the grass was wet;
Hurry, old clock, I want to be grown."
But the clock ticked on, "Not yet, not yet."

A young girl stood in the same hall door,
Watching her lover go down the way
He had gone so often, but nevermore
Would come again; then, smiling gay,
She turned to the old clock muttering there,
And said with the slightest, subtlest trace
Of her once imperious childish air,
Mixed with her maidenly charm and grace,
"Hurry, old clock, you are so slow;
Though both of us thought you far too fast,
As we often have, a moment ago.
Oh, if meetings would only last!
Already I long his face to see;
Let the swift moons rise and the swift suns set,
And bring back my darling quick to me."
But the clock ticked on, "Not yet, not yet."

A sad-faced woman leant in her chair,
In the self-same door at the close of day,
And still in its wonted corner there
Grimly the old clock ticked away.
The woman turned from the fading skies
To the only voice in the lonely hall,
And said, with reproach in her weary eyes,
"The same old song since I was small!
Hurry, old clock-you are so slow,
And my heart impatient beats so fast.
The time is tedious: I long to go,
Oh, if partings were only past,
And we might meet in that dreamland blest
Where all my troubles I might forget,
Clasped once more to my darling's breast!"
But the clock ticked on, "Not yet, not yet."

By Julia Stockton Dinsmore

"THAT'S FOR REMEMBERANCE"

SWEET scent of wild Kentucky Mint!
 The poignant perfume brings to me
Scenes that the rolling years imprint
 On memory's scrolls indelibly;
The shout of youth, the laugh of mirth,
 All the glad music loved of old,
The breath of lips long sealed in earth,
 The clasp of hands long still and cold.

How oft our childish feet have trod
 Along the winding, rippling creek,
The mint among the bluegrass sod,
 Jumping from rock to rock to seek
The water snake eluding still
 The swift pursuit, the eager throw,
And with hereditary skill
 Escaping to the pool below.

And then the foolish crawfish peered
 From shelter of his slimy stone,
And flounced along till, harried, jeered,
 We pounced upon him for our own;

And then our little henchman bore,
With wily, woolly head, elate.
The prize off in the gourd whose store
Of worms and crickets was our bait.

That ancient mint, I smell it yet,
 Quintessence of or sport and fun,
Trampled and tangled, bruised and wet
Most Fragrant when most rod upon;
 We fished with many a fancy fling,
With many a jest and give and boast;
 The little henchman with his string
And pinhook always caught the most.

Oh, sweet scent in after time!
 When our two horses close abreast,
Rattling the rocks in clashing chime
 Among the mint their sure hoofs pressed.
Mid-summer then, and to the leaves
 The added sweetness of the flowers.
But tenderest memory mutely grieves,
 No more, no more-the rest is ours.

All the rich life forever past
 Breathes in his perfume's affluence,
Hope's vanished vision vague and vast,
 The spirit's long-lost innocence
All that death's subtle mystery
 Can dumbly show or darkly hint;
No garden rosemary for me,
 But springs of wild Kentucky mint.

By Julia Stockton Dinsmore

MEMORY

Once in a home whose memories yet
Console a lone heart heavy laden,
There lived a child, a perfect pet
From cherub babe to budding maiden;
Child of sweet looks and sweeter ways,
The kind foreboding nurses know
And quaintly call, "too good to raise."
No wonder that we loved her so,
We cherished her, caressed and kissed her,
The household joy, the little sister

A wild-wood flower, unsought, unknown,
Perished before its perfect blooming
Whose fragrance from the dim past blown
Life's twilight hour is still perfuming
I could not covet gift or grace
Of hers whose joy was always mine,
But oft I envy her place
In earth's calm breast and memory's shrine:
How fair she seems adown times' vista-
Still young, still dear, the little sister!

Our Father many mansions hath,
For Heaven is large as love, not merit,
And thither throng by many a path
The blessed children who inherit-,
But were it measured straight foursquare
With golden reed to great white throne,
By best Beatitude an heir
She would but come into her own;
The gates of pearl could not resist her-
The pure in heart, the little sister.

But words are vain; they falter, fail,
Leave the long silence still unbroken,
Her home is now within the vail
Where mortal love is never spoken;
Yet in the cup of that life's bliss
The drop that makes it overflow
May be a memory of this,
And she may recollect and know-
Know how we loved her, mourned her, missed her,
The early lost, the little sister

By Julia Stockton Dinsmore

FRIENDSHIP RENEWED

DEAR friend, both old and new, when Fate her spell
  Cast o'er our love in childhood's happy hour,
  Entranced, like Sleeping Beauty in the bower
It lay till Time annulled her witchery fell.
Now waking, young as then, its dazed eyes dwell
  On faces wan, that only Memory's power
Can brighten with the looks that were their dower
  In the far past that she recalls so well.
What treasure-trove this friendship old and rare!
Our love may be like that strange Eastern flower
  That life suspending holds its fragrant breath
Till, trailer blossoms strewed and garden bare,
  With tender care revived from feigned death,
It sheds its sweetness on the wintry air.

By Julia Stockton Dinsmore

Chapter One:

Tributes to the Memory of Dr. Martin Luther King, Jr.

The Kentucky Dr. King State Commission, in collaboration with the Governor's Office of Minority Empowerment, sponsors an annual writing and visual arts contest as a way for Kentucky students to honor the memory of Dr. Martin Luther King, Jr. The 2016 Dr. King memorial theme was "Making Lives Matter". On January 14, 2016, these four students from the St. Pius X School seventh grade class were recognized for their written expression: Jenna Danneman, Sky Morris, J.J. Kampinga, and Tre Lohre. Jenna, Sky, and J.J. received first, second, and third place honors for their poems. Tre was a second place winner in the essay division. All were invited to shake hands with the Lieutenant Governor and to have photos taken as they received their award in Frankfort at the Dr. Thomas Clark History Center.

On January 17, Lauren Davey was recognized locally for her essay as part of a Diocesan memorial tribute to Dr. King. Her essay was selected from all middle school entries in the Covington Diocese. In the presence of the Most Reverend Bishop Foys, Lauren shared her essay, "Martin's Dream for the Future, My Dream for Tomorrow".

My Hero, Dr. King

One man with many big dreams,
When times were ripping at the seams.

He may have been an old town pastor,
But he became a freedom and peace master.

He mended the U.S.
and let freedom ring
With the last name Luther King.

A real person
who cared about every life;
He had two daughters, a son, a wife.

Mended the U.S. and created
A more peaceful nation.
With love and meaning
In equality reformation.

He chose love and equality over hate;
1963, August 28 was a very special date.

He said only four words
That will change my life forever:
"I have a dream."
Forget those words?
Never!

You don't have to fight
to let freedom ring.
You may know this man
As Dr. Martin Luther King.

by Jenna Danneman

Dr. King: In His Words

Martin Luther King, Jr.
All lives matter.
Keep moving forward.
If you can't fly then run,
 if you can't run then walk,
 if you can't walk then crawl.
Non-violence is the principle of love.
Gaining our rightful place
  means we must not be guilty of wrongful deeds.

Love is the only force capable
 of transforming an enemy into a friend.
Injustice anywhere is a threat to justice everywhere.
Violence multiplies violence.
Everything we see is a shadow cast by that which we do not see.
Stick with love; hate is too great a burden to bear.

Men are caught in
  an inescapable network of mutuality.
A　riot is the language of the unheard.
The time is always right to do what is right.
True peace is not merely the absence of tension;
 it is the presence of justice.
Every man of humane convictions must decide
 on the protest that best suits his convictions,
 but we must all protest.
Right, temporally defeated, is stronger than evil triumphant.

by Tre Lohre

The fights, the violence,
the silence of the children who await to be free;
there are so many good people in the world, better than me.
Their voices are heard from miles around,
lots of joy in their heart they found.
The persecutors, the evildoers of the sick world;
he wished the good people ruled,
People like Martin Luther King,
Who tried every little thing.
He took a stand and fought for freedom,
Sadly the people didn't take the love he gave them.
He tried to say that all lives matter,
but then there was chatter,
What if he said a speech,
But then we would have to reach,
go the extra mile,
Be the man with the smile.
He made a difference,
but there was an interference.
He was killed; it seems like all the good people are,
And Martin said, "A riot is the language of the unheard."

by Sky Morris

Martin Luther King Jr.
Shared the idea that all lives matter.
Not even a bullet to his body could shatter
the immortal dream of
total freedom
from the manacles of segregation,
from the chains of discrimination.
He said,
"A man should not be judged by the color of his skin,
But by the content of his character."
He said great things,
helped many people.
He bridged the gap
between whites and blacks.

by JJ Kampinga

Martin Luther King Jr.
He had a dream
Black people would be the same.
For that dream he had to be a believer.

by Jared Simon

Life.
Beautiful. Happy,
Playing, Eating, Sleeping,
White, Black, Respect,
Running, Crying, Loving,
Precious, Marvelous
You

by Lily Shay

Martin Luther had a speech
that he liked to preach.
"I have a dream" he said,
and people started to believe what he read.
But still people bled.
Blacks were not treated fairly.
And whites said, "I'm sorry", rarely.
He believed that all lives matter.
Martin Luther's dream would never shatter!

by Skyllar Jacocks

Why Do Lives Matter?

Why do lives matter? They matter because we are all created in the likeness and image of Jesus Christ. Even the sick and the poor. Even the old and elderly. Even the young and the unborn. It does not matter the color of your skin or your home country. We all are made in the image of God.

We can make all lives matter by including everyone. Even if someone looks different, we should not exclude them. It would make them feel disappointed and that they are not "good" enough when we really are all equal. If you see someone on the playground that looks lonely, go up and ask if they want to play with you or your group.

Life is important. We should always protect life no matter what the circumstances are. Everyone is created in the image and likeness of God. We will not stop until all are being treated fairly.

As Martin Luther King Jr. said "The time is always right to do what is right." This means that you always should do what is right. Even if it is not popular or "cool", you should still do it. Are you willing to include everyone?

by Tre Lohre

Dr. King

In church he used to sing,
Oh good ole Dr. King

He clearly stated all lives matter;
Without him
African Americans would be shattered

He said love trumps hate;
He didn't like to discriminate

In church he used to sing,
Oh good ole Dr. King

He will not discriminate;
He had no room to hate

He was a victim of discrimination;
He lead a black nation

In church he used to sing,
Oh good ole Dr. King

by Elliot Bent

Martin
Great, brave
Leading, daring, preaching
People, genius, Martin
Smart, awesome
Good

by Charlie Smith

Dr. Martin Luther King Jr.
Tall, Peacemaker
Loving, Protecting, Caring
Making lives matter,
Leader, Preacher, Activist
Saving , Controlling, Outstanding
Caring, Inspirational
Freedom

by Brayden Sanning

                    Life, Respected, Unique
                Breathing, Speaking, Living
                    Whites, People, Blacks
                 Leading, Caring, Learning
                     Loved, Joyful Person

                               by Ella Weaver

Freedom
Precious, Exclusive
Appreciating, Loving, Protecting
Leader, Preacher, Humanitarian
Activist, Leading, Changing
Justifying, Courageous, Committed
Martin Luther King, Jr.

by Trey Gronotte

That blacks wouldn't have to scream,
"Equality, justice, and fairness."
All they wanted was awareness.
Martin Luther believed all lives matter,
Blacks' hope would never shatter,
Whites persecuted blacks,
But Martin Luther's word impacts,
Words laced with only love,
Speaking of things blacks could only dream of.

by Corinne Laws

MLK Poem

Dr. King was great and brave
With that, the consequences were grave.
Dr. King stopped segregation
Because that was not why God made creation.
The person to help stop racism was Dr. King.
Dr. King was assassinated in the spring;
Dr. King has died.

Everyone would need a new guide.

by Ethan Wever

Martin Luther King Jr.

Martin Luther fought for rights,
He brought light to the other side.
He took a long ride
Just to make things right.
They had him falling to his knees
Because he had a dream
Of people being free;
Blacks and whites, all alike
To stand up for the fight
Of equal rights.
To soar above
The laws of injustice,
Trying to make things right
For all humanity
For the future of our world,
So we may be free
From the evil that consumes us;
To turn us to the people we were supposed to be.
Martin Luther King, Jr.

by Anne-Marie Wright

He loved to live
He loved to love
He stood up for right
He was the light
He was very bright
Even though he wasn't always right, he would fight
His name was Martin Luther King, Jr. and he was a hero.

by Isabelle Bennett

Martin Luther King, Jr.
Hopeful, Patient
Inspiring, Outstanding, Unwavering
Always thinking about others
Uniting, Teaching, Forgiving
Humble, Influential
Martin Luther King, Jr.

by Maggie Smith

Martin Luther King

He was a hero
A leader
A speaker
A man of great courage
And wise.
A coach
And a believer
Peacemaker and preacher
And equal we all are in his eyes.

by Logan Finke

He had a dream, a great big dream
The dream was very extreme
He let people hear what was on his mind
And people became very unkind
But he would not let them bring him down
So he preached the right thing now
Now that everyone understands what he said
Then the speech spread very fast.

by Ava Quigley

Dr. King

Hero, Kind, Friendly,
Peacemaking, Protesting segregation,
Saver, Role Model, Leader,
Boycotting, Dreaming, Ministering,
Brave, Historic, Preacher

by Ross Lux

Making Lives Matter

Martin Luther King Jr.
Intelligent, Self-Sacrificing, Dreaming, Fighting,
Making Lives Matter
Rights, March on Washington,
Political Change, Marching, Fighting,
Brave, Loving, Freedom

by Jacob Robke

Freedom! "Let it ring," said Dr. King.
The bells go ring, cling, ding,
That means freedom rings.
"Ring, cling, ding," said Dr. King;
Listen closely and you will hear that ding;
The ding will glisten.
Don't just ring your own bell; ring others' bells
Because everyone matters, black or white;
So listen together, we can reach new heights.
WE can make freedom ring!

by Michael Thiel

Makes lives matter
Atlanta, Georgia January 15, 1929
Remarkable
Tennessee
I have a dream
Not neglecting

Leader
United
Thoughtful
Helps others
Energetic
Ready to fight

Kind person
Intelligent
Nobel Peace Prize
Gave his life

Justice
Righteous

by Kierstin Haas

Martin Luther King Jr.

Dr. King: Heroic
Brave, Debating,
Boycotting,
Changing segregation
Equality, Hatred,
Marching, Striding,
Leading Unfairness,
Justice, Legend

by Claire Edgington

Dr. MLK Jr.

Dr. MLK Jr. freed African Americans.
Now there is no segregation.
Sadly, though there is still racism.
Some cops are very unfair.
He is a role model,
MLK and no segregation.

by Ryan Bosch

Dr. King

Kind, Smart
Fighting, Trying
Equalizing
Pastor
African American
Friend
Helping, Loving
Preaching
Friendly, Fair
Martin

by Calista Solo

Dr. King

Some kings sat down with luxury.
 Our king stood strong,
     stood proud,
         stood tall.
Dr. King had a dream
that all people will be treated
with peace and love.
He was like a dove.
Dr. King was a peacemaker,
not a peace-breaker.
He loved all, he stopped brawls.
He was a brave man.
 I was a huge fan.

by Jass Brewer

Making Lives Matter

MLK is still making lives matter,
Not even Earl Ray's bullet could shatter
His dream.

Martin King had a very big dream,
And at that time Ray was planning his theme.

He gave a well known speech,
It taught everyone in reach.

Suddenly this famous man died,
Everyone hid, far and wide.

Although his legacy still lives on,
The presence of his life is forever gone.

Martin Luther was a brave man,
He has been one from the day he began.

Even though Martin Luther King Jr. is missed,
We still remember him as if it were written on our wrist.

by Madelyn Gordon

Martin Luther King Jr.

Martin Luther was a good man
He thought up a really good plan
Things were bad so he made them right
But he didn't put anyone in fright
He never got in a fight
Martin knew this was all wrong
So he had to grow his group strong.

by Riley Jordan

Dr. King was a very caring,
loving man.
He wanted little kids
to hold hands,
No matter the color of their skin.
That is why everyone liked (him)
in many different ways.

by Ashton Isler

Life Matters

Dr. King chose love over hate,
There is no debate
That all lives matter;
His heart will not shatter
For there will be no delay
That we will stand together on this day.
For he once started at zero
Now he is our hero.

by Abby Powers

Martin

Smart, Intelligent
Caring, Loving, Sharing
Wonderful, Genius, Fighter
Teaching, Preaching, Inspiring
Strong, Champion, Freedom

by Luke T

"Injustice Anywhere is a Threat to Justice Everywhere"

When African Americans weren't treated right,
Martin Luther King Jr. clenched his fists tight.
With protests and boycotts, he changed the world.
Emotions of both black and white people swirled.
He made people understand
of the oppression at hand.
So that they could see
that all races should be free!
Injustice is a threat to justice, that's what he thought was true.
He would stick to these ideas for his whole life like glue.
Making all people's lives matter was his goal,
And he made some people realize that right down to their soul.
But even today, there is racism on Earth,
So we should bring Martin's ideas back to birth.

by Collin Gerwe

Martin Luther King Jr.
Heroic, brave,
amazing, loving, caring,
leader, speeches, freedom, preacher
willing, inspiring, persevering,
justice, graceful.
Making Lives Matter.

by Emily Brennen

Martin Luther

He fought against segregation
He put a lot of people out of depression.
He made a lot of people mad
But most people were glad.
He was jailed a few times
None of them were crimes.
He gave his famous "I Have a Dream" speech
His ultimate goal was to teach.
He walked hundreds of miles to make a difference
But he didn't lose a bit of his brilliance.
He made lives matter
Yet his dream didn't shatter
For things to become fair.
King

by Andrew Bosch

Dr. King thought of an idea:
If the world was right,
It wouldn't matter, black or white.
All people are equal.
And all lives matter.

by Reece Murphy

His Dream Lives On

He approached the crowd without any fear,
He had a fire in his heart he held very dear.

No one could stop him; he wanted to make lives matter,
He showed us great courage that no one could shatter.

He started preaching out his word,
Which will never ever be unheard.

Everyone got chills up their back,
For this was no drama act.

He marched with much pride,
Until just then MLK died.

Even though you cannot see him anymore,
Martin Luther King got what he was fighting for.

Dr. King's dream still lives on,
Even though he is gone.

by Paige Neuhaus

Martin Luther King Jr. Poem

"Let no man pull you low enough to hate him."
He was a very great man,
so nice--
Some didn't understand.
Used his words, not his hands;
Spoke about freedom and how it rang.
He spoke about what he felt was right,
And he didn't need to start a fight.

by Macy Feagan

Dr. King

Fair, just,
amazing, caring, loving
king, man, love
nice, wonderful
sharing, carrying, king
peace

by Ava Hassan

Martin's Dream for the Future, My Dream for Tomorrow

Lauren Davey

Dr. Martin Luther King, Jr. had a dream for the future. He said, "No one should be judged by the color of their skin but by the content of their character." His dream for the future is very important to me. It shows that each person should be treated fairly, and no one should be excluded because they are different. Instead of judging people by appearance, discover who they are inside, their inner strength and character. Then we have a better idea of people as individuals.

Dr. King's dream had a major impact upon our country. By speaking out about what he wanted for the future, he helped change the way that people thought about African Americans. White business owners began to take down their "whites only" and "colored" signs. Schools allowed children of all races to attend. African Americans were allowed to vote freely without fear. Views about people of color changed. Many whites realized that there was a need for fairness and equality.

Despite these positive changes, we need to encourage people to do more. We cannot let the color of someone's skin affect how they are treated in society. Our job is to inspire people to be respectful and to make our country even better.

Even at my school, kids are not always treated fairly. Some of my classmates are the last to be chosen for a game or as a partner for project. To make Dr. King's dream a reality, I can work with people who are not usually picked first or to invite someone new to sit with me at lunch

In my community, I can volunteer at missions and soup kitchens and talk to lonely people there. I can serve by giving my time, being with them, bringing them some happiness. My dream is similar to Martin's dream. I want all people to feel happy for who they are and to feel welcome anywhere they go.

Dr. King had a dream that everyone would unite and realize that we are all equal. Tall or small, white or black, brunette or blonde, we are all the same inside. We each have a personality and feelings that need to be considered. We all have an equal chance to succeed. That is my dream for the world today.

Dr. King

Dr. King had to say,
all his rights had slipped away.
While whites were living the life,
Martin Luther was having strife.
He thought segregation was the worst,
he may have thought they were cursed.
Segregation was extreme,
but Martin Luther said "I have a dream!"

Anonymous

MADE HISTORY
AMAZING
RESTLESS
TACTICAL
INVOLVED IN THE BOYCOTT
NICE.

LOVING
UTTER GREATNESS
TEACHING OTHERS
HOPEFUL FOR END OF SEGREGATION
EAGER TO MAKE A CHANGE IN SOCIETY
RICH IN SPIRIT.

by Grant Montelisciani

Making Lives Matter

Martin Luther King Jr. changed the future.
Martin Luther fought against discrimination.
Martin made today a good new haven.
Martin Luther was very peaceful.
Everything he did was to help the people.

You may know his great speech.
Very inspirational, his speech was to preach.
The speech had a name which was, "I Have a Dream"
He wanted everyone to know that we are all on the same team.

Martin Luther King showed love instead of hate.
He made this land truly great.
Martin had a dream that everyone would stand
united together in this wonderful land.
Although Martin Luther has passed on,
MKL Jr. made this day in age a beautiful dawn.

Anonymous

Martin Luther King Jr.

He started preaching about equal rights when something went wrong.

Rosa Parks and a bus driver weren't getting along.

Rosa Parks got arrested arguing with him.

Apparently the white people thought it was a sin.

Martin Luther King Jr. had the world in his mind.

Being fair, and equal, he wanted everyone to be kind.

He wanted his children to have a better life than that.

So he started doing something about it, to make things right.

He put his life in danger; it was such a fright.

Once he achieved his goal, he thought lives mattered.

Everyone who adored him was flattered.

He did it, though; he made things fair.

He put his love and effort into it. He really did care!

by Aria Meier

Making Lives Matter

He was against discrimination
He helped to change the entire nation
He strived to make the world more peaceful
And gain equal rights for his people
He helped others
One after another
He had a speech to share
For his cause – he did care
Martin loved and showed no hate
And that was his characteristic trait
Martin taught what he knew
In order to help me and you.

by Maddie Maciejewski

Martin Luther King
The Inspirer

He taught me to give my all,
To make peace and to stop brawls;
To treat every individual with dignity
And mourn for others with sympathy.
He clearly stated
"ALL LIVES MATTER."
No dreams deserve to be shattered.
All people count,
No matter how big their checking account.
Do not judge other people by how they look.
He taught all are equal;
Everyone is coequal.
We are all important in the end,
And that is why we should all be friends.
All Lives Matter.

by Jaden Siemer

We All Matter

Martin was the one
that gave African Americans equal rights;
He showed what we stood for,
that we all matter.
Even though it was dangerous
he still spoke out.
And in his famous speech
he was willing to shout.
Now everyone is equal and are all friends,
And it will stay that way until the end.
He encouraged people to speak out, too.
Like Rosa Parks, that was a brave thing to do.
He has some nicknames, such as MLK,
And he was here to save the day.
Sadly, he was assassinated,
but was very brave,
The lives of his children he did save.
All days we remember Dr. King,
We remember to let freedom ring.

by Annabelle Sunday

Life Matters

Dr. King chose love over hate,
there is no debate.
That all lives matter.
For there will be no delay
that we will stand together on this day.
For he once started at zero,
now he is our hero.

by Abby Powers

DR. KING

Kind, Smart
Fighting, Trying, Equalizing
Pastor, African American, Friend
Helping, Loving, Preaching
Friendly, Fair
MARTIN

by Calista Solo

DR. KING

Fair, Just, Amazing
Caring, Loving, King,
Man, Love, Sharing,
Glaring, King, Nice
Wonderful, Peace

by Ava Hassan

Dr. King

He was brought upon an age of depression,
Where he made a major impression.
He wanted everyone to see,
The greatness of equality.
He taught that we shouldn't do wrong,
That we need hope to stay strong.
He tried to end all discrimination,
Until that day of his assassination.
So let freedom ring today,
So we remember MLK.

by Drew Kent

Martin my friend, even though we will never see you again, we will always remember you for all of the things you could teach and do. You taught people that there was no cause to act like black people were against all laws. You taught us all to care, you taught us to share even though you got caught in quite a snare. You said everyone should be equal, but now there's a new sequel. Some people are changing back into their old ways like lots of people acted in the darker days. Some people will never change, but I know you will always be there to teach, tell, share, and care.

by Jordan Gillum

Do you know my friend?

He made lives matter until his end.

He was a light to those in the dark of segregation.

He took a stand without hesitation.

I wish he were here because people are being careless again.

They are killing others without any thought.

Do they all just have a blind spot?

All lives matter; just ask my friend.

He would always comprehend.

His name was Martin and he believed

That we all matter, you and me.

by Claire Dunham

Dr. Martin Luther King Jr.

Martin Luther was a wonderful man,
Was very kind and very grand,
Loved all the people in the world,
But suddenly his life was twirled.
Such a passion for world peace,
Then he gave an incredible speech.
"I Have a Dream" is very popular,
Very smart and very proper,
He started out as a great preacher,
Could have been a very good teacher,
Continued to grow,
It wasn't very slow;
Not nervous to show he cared a lot.
Did he give up? No, he did not!
We'll still remember Martin Luther
Helped our country to a better future.
Segregation is mostly gone;
Now our world is as bright as dawn.

by Zach Tucker

Have you seen my friend?
He changed a lot of lives.
He fought against segregation,
and changed the nation,
without any disguises.

He said "I have a dream."
With a gleam in his eye,
he never stopped believing
he could achieve anything.
He just had to keep on going.

My friend Martin Luther King,
fought 'til the end.
He said, "Let's bring love, not hate"
and always look around the bend.

by Lauren Davey

Dr. Martin Luther King Jr.

All people do matter.
Without just one person, it wouldn't be the same.
It isn't okay to judge by the color of skin.
It is what is on the inside that truly matters.
All people are unique in their own way,
Everyone should be treated the same.
If everyone were kind to each other,
It would make a big change.
Standing up for what is right takes courage.
As it is the time to always do what is right.
All lives matter,
So we should all be treated the same.
Let no one pull you down,
because there should be no hate.

by Hope McNickle

MLK JR.

Martin Luther King, Jr.
He was a great man,
he didn't throw cans
He was indifferent
that people were different.
Segregation was no fable;
he put that fact right out
on the table.
But most of all, he showed
that all lives matter,
by making a clatter.

By Chris Mason

Have you seen my friend?
He wasn't there just to defend.
He changed the nation,
Without hesitation.
He made every life matter
                until the end;
He was the new trend.
He stopped segregation,
It was a sensation.
He said "I have a dream,"
It was supreme.
The black and white signs on
the street.
He made theme go away;
it was pretty sweet.

by Olivia Maschinot

Martin Luther King, Jr.

Anonymous

Martin Luther fought for rights;
He brought light to the other side.
He took a long ride
Just to make things right.
They had him falling on his knees
Because he had a dream of people being free;
Black and white, all alike
To stand up for the fight
Of equal rights;
To soar above
The laws of injustice
Trying to make things right
For all humanity —
For the future of our world —
That we may be free
From the evil that consumes us;
To turn us to the people
We are meant to be:
Martin Luther King

All lives matter
this is true, God thinks of
me and you. Dr. King thought
the same way, he thought like
that every single day. Believe
that this is no lie. No one
is better than you or
I. We are equal
in God's eyes,
To know that he had to
be very wise. Dr. King wanted to
make a change, and lots of people thought that
he was   strange. But lots thought that   he had a
point, there   was no other option so they   became joint
Soon most   of the nation believed in   his cause,
But they were   a peaceful protest so   they obeyed
the laws.   Then came the March on   Washington,
for their   campaign this would be   a huge win!
"Lot freedom ring", said
Martin Luther King."Let
us all live   in harmony,
peace for   you and me.
Let freedom   ring, let
freedom ring,   let it ring."
said Dr. King.   today is the
day that we all   sing, in honor
of Martin Luther   King. Wherever
people fight to be free, his   name is remembered
with dignity. That's all I have   to say, except that we're alive
like this because of what Dr.   Martin Luther King had to say.

Chapter Two:
Just for Fun

Slightly the ball is tapped from one striker to another,
putting the ball in play.
Quickly, the striker passes to the right,
confusing the behind defenders.
Beautifully, the ball is kicked, past the goalkeeper
penetrating the goal.
Excitedly, the offense runs down the field,
rousing the whole crowd watching.

by Collin Gerwe

Quickly the ball was hit
speeding near the net.
Hurrying, the opponent rushes to the ball.
Hitting the ball, he almost misses.
Quickly, the ball flies.
Flying, the ball goes in.
Slowly, the ball bounces,
missing the opponent's net.

by Tre Lohre

Luxuriously, the princess got a ride
to the kingdom.
Skipping, the princess went inside
Magically, she appeared.

by Olivia Maschinot

Slowly the ball rolled,
making its way to the goal.
Skillfully, the goalie dived,
trying to stop the ball.
Finally, the ball crossed the line
igniting the crowd.
Quickly the fans run on to the field
lifting the star player.

by Drew Kent

Nervously dribbling down the court,
Eyeing the other players,
Fiercely driving to the basket,
Cheering crowds ringing in their ears;
Aggressively pushing the other players aside,
The ticking of the final seconds of the game
Gracefully shooting the ball
Roaring crowds are heard
as the ball enters the hoop!

by Anne-Marie Wright

The Drew Song

My name is Drew
and I like beef stew
I always day dream
and my favorite color's green.
I like alpacas but I don't like llamas.
I like science but I don't like drama!

by Drew Kent

Smoothly the golfer
drew back the golf club,
preparing to swing.
Swiftly the golfer
swung his club,
knocking the ball
into the air.

by Chris Mason

Quickly, the time drops down,
passing the ball
in a continuous motion.
Swiftly, the ball is stolen.
Shooting the ball!

by Andrew Bosch

Mournfully, the wolf howls,
looking at the moon glowing.
Happily, the little wolf
would find it.

by Ross Lux

Quickly, the ball is passed around,
finding a player free.
Gently, the player receives the ball,
taking it down the field,
Carefully completing a move,
running past a defender.
Finally, the player shoots,
scoring the final goal!

by Lauren Davey

Sadly, the dog missed the Frisbee.
Jumping, the dog tried again.
Happily, the dog reached the Frisbee.
Running through the brush,
he was lost.
Flying out of the woods,
Then pausing,
the dog fell asleep.

by Grant Montelisciani

Swiftly, the player dribbles
down the court,

Continuing the dribble,
dribble, dribble,

Bounce, bounce, bounce of
the ball.

Willingly, the player passes it
off,

Signaling the others to score.

by Reece Murphy

The Mysterious Creature
Anonymous

I climb
a tree to see it better.
It growled
and scratched the tree.
It took a jump
chasing after me.
I tried
to get a better look
at its furry, furry face.
It was
a big black dog
who never had a haircut.
It licked me.

The Dog and the Frog

by Tre Lohre

There once was a dog;
    it played all day;
    met a frog
      and they ran away.
They played in the woods.
      They played in the field.
They played all day;
    Then they lay
    down to sleep,
The dog and the frog.

Beach Poem
Anonymous

I walk to the beach three miles away.
Once there, I can smell the salt.
Jumping in the sand,
I feel the grit between my toes,
    the sun beating down,
the water cold at first, but warm in a while.
No clouds in the sky, beach balls flying, people smiling.
Cold ice cream to cool me down; a sunset at the end of the day;
as I lie on a towel facing the sky, I can see stars flying by.

Giggling with Gators

We both stood in the marsh, shocked that we had seen each other. So I walked forward -- I thought I'd tell a joke. As I stepped forward, I said "Why did the chicken cross the road?" Then as I entertained him, a roar of laughter came ashore. We laughed forever and ever.

by Michael Thiel

Dogs
Wagging tails
Cold noses
Wet kisses
Long walks—
A family's best friend.

by Maggie Smith

Rambunctious Art
by Maggie Smith

Rambunctious art

makes my heart flutter

then overwhelms me;

My heart beats faster

My eyes open wider

The colors, the beauty, the surprise

Of it all

Life is art;

Art is life.

Chapter Three: Life and Faith

God

God is always there and always cares.
Show him respect and he will protect.
He will give you love from above
in the form of a dove.
Praise him in many ways.

by Charlie Smith

No matter what, always be nice.
That is the best advice.
Always smile because there is tomorrow,
even though it might be hard to show.
Life may be tough,
even though it's rough.
Sometimes you just gotta hold it,
even if it will be hard to admit.

by Maddie Maciejewski

God-
amazing,
beautiful,
blessing,
forgiving,
praising,
Cross,
Eucharist,
blood,
rosary,
thanking,
watching,
praying,
outstanding,
unbelievable
FATHER

by Brooke Murphy

SALVATION

Jesus is my Savior.
He granted me salvation.
He gave his life for all people-
hypocrites, sinners, blasphemers.
He loved them all.
He reached out to them
with a gentle hand and a loving gaze.
They turn to him, wanting to feel accepted.
And he gives them exactly what they want.

by Corinne Laws

Trust in God, you will
never regret it. He
will help you a lot
and you will never
forget it. He will be
by your side, so just sit back and enjoy the ride, for he will be your almighty guide. He loves us all, big or small. Just keep on praying he will give you a call, because he is the greatest of all. He knows and loves just everyone, son or daughter. If we trust in Him
we will have eternal life.
We will all stop and put
down our guns and fists.
We'll use peace to work
things out, and live our
Christian life. Helping all
people even if they do not
call. We must be there
to help others with care.

by Reece Murphy

Jesus Christ

When it was time, everyone was so excited!
This was the time that God and human were reunited.
God gave Jesus a mission;
 He would prove there was only one true God!
But everyone thought he was a little odd.
He sacrificed his life to save our sins.
But when Jesus dies, that is when everlasting life begins.
There are a lot of people who don't believe in Jesus.
They're missing a lot if they don't believe
in the one who freed us!
I know I believe in Christ!
What about you?

by Aria Meier

Easter Time

by Emily Brennen

We raced down the stairs.
Mom and Dad were there,
but we didn't care.

We hunt and hunt.
To get eggs, I do stunts.

I win.
Eggs filled my bin.

We open our eggs
quickly
A laugh slips out
wickedly.

Coming of Age

Age is deadly.
It's a cage that brings out rage.
Age is a page
that you can flip.
Age can drip
and taint.
Age ain't fun.
Age is as deadly as a gun.

by Ethan Wever

Feelings, they are everywhere.
They're up and down,
they're all around.
Why do I feel this way,
thinking about it all day?
I'm confused but amused.
Why do I feel used?
But the thing is:
I'm supposed to feel this way,
'cause I'm no whiz.
I'm a teen;
there's no in-between.
I'm not supposed to know.
I'll start off slow.
But that's why you're here,
for me to hear.
You are my parents,
And there's no in-between.

by Anne-Marie Wright

Teenagers

Anonymous

We're growing up; what can I say?
No parents can stand to bear these days.
We are getting tall and mean.
Thinking of ourselves as kings and queens,
thinking we rule the world as teens.
Always on our phones,
not knowing how to talk to people
socially, on our own.
The teenage years can be the worst or the best
depending on what you make of the quest.

The Sunset
by Skyllar Jacocks

The beautiful sunset colored the sky—
a variety of colors to please the eye.
Purple, yellow, green; blue, purple, pink.
It looked like heaven—
the sun shining down, suddenly disappearing.
It dazzled and awed for a few fleeting minutes
– brief but amazing.
So, live like a sunset.
Be many colors; be amazing!

WINTER
Anonymous

One snowy night there was a little girl who asked her mother "What's so great about winter?" Her mother smiled and replied:

"You can make snowballs, angels, and snowmen. There are reindeers, elves, Santa, too; hot chocolate, beautiful fires, and roasted nuts. There are lights, evergreens, and cookies, happiness, joy and laughter. There is a spirit that casts over town, puts everyone in a good mood. So don't you frown. Winter is fun, exciting, and love. That is what winter is, honey."

And the little girl grinned a big grin and said "I love winter now!"

Summer

Anonymous

I was taking a ride on a boat
enjoying the glistening water.

We glide through the water,
the blazing sun shining on my face.

The breeze cuts through the sky like knives,
sunlight cascading down like a waterfall.

The Song

As I walked down the street,
I wanted to go to sleep.
I was tired and weak.
Can't a body get a little sleep?

by Isabelle Bennett

Deep Space

by Jaden Siemer

I gaze up into the stars.
I can see a beautiful Mars.
As I look into space
it is such a faraway place.
I wish I could travel up there
and go all the way up into the air.
I want to go up and look down at Earth
and see the humongous girth.
I want to see the moon up close
and be the only one that knows
the beauty of space.

How to Find Happiness

To find happiness you must rent a tent.
Then you must find a cent and be lent some cement.
The cement will be used for your field event.
While at the field event I underwent some circumvent.
The track event was on the way.
While I was watching for the track event I sat in my rent-a-tent,
With my cent that I bought my cement.
While watching the event I got in an argument.
So now I can't tell you how to find happiness,
but if you rent a tent and
Spend a cent on cement
At a field event,
During the track event
You will find happiness.

by Michael Thiel

Fearful Encounter

Stopping dead in my tracks
stunned by
the dull red eyes that glimmer
in the night.
Fear overcomes me.

My body is stiff.
My breathing heavy.
My heart is beating faster, faster.

The animal stares right at me.
He lowers his body ready to attack
As a low growl escapes his mouth.

Fear begins to eat me alive.
Then suddenly,
the animal runs
back into the wilderness.
Relief fills my body.

Even to this day the memory still strikes me-
shocked
that I came face to face with a wolf.

by Anne-Marie Wright

```
                                    shell shell shell
                                 shell shell shell shell shell
                                shell  shell  shell  shell  shell
              head head         shell shell shell shell shell shell shell
          head head head head   shell shell shell shell shell shell shell shell
          head head head head   shell shell shell shell shell shell shell shell shell
        head head head head head    shell leg leg leg shell shell shell leg leg leg shell shell
        neck neck neck neck neck    shell leg leg leg shell shell shell leg leg leg shell shell
           neck neck neck neck shell leg leg leg shell shell shell leg leg leg shell  shell
              neck neck neckshell/leg leg leg shell shell shell leg leg leg shell  shell
                                leg leg leg leg   shell   shell leg leg leg leg shell
                                leg leg leg leg                 leg leg leg leg
                                leg leg leg leg                 leg leg leg leg
                                leg leg leg leg                 leg leg leg leg
                                leg leg leg leg                 leg leg leg leg
                                leg leg leg leg                 leg leg leg leg
                                 foot foot foot foot             foot foot foot foot
                                foot foot foot foot foot        foot foot foot foot foot
```

Chapter Four: Homeroom 701

Ghosts
by Riley Jordan

Ghosts,
Scary, Creepy
Screaming, Scaring, Spine-chilling,
Zombies, Headless Horsemen, Skeletons,
Horrifying, Shocking, Alarming,
Deathlike, Risking,
Bats.

Puppies
by Annabelle Sunday

Puppies,
Playful, Small,
Barking, Fetching, Chasing,
Boxer, Great Dane, German Shepherd,
Sleeping, Guarding, Helping,
Smart, Big,
Dogs.

Dogs
by Maddie Maciejewski

Dogs,
Playing, running,
Caring, loving, friendly,
Buddy, fuzz ball, lapdog, stress reliever,
Barking, cuddling, sniffing,
Heartwarming, quirky,
Puppy.

Volleyball

by Aria Meier

Volleyball
Awesome, Fun,
Passing, Setting, Hitting,
Outsider, Middle, Libero,
Serving, Shuffling, Shouting,
Cool, Great,

Halloween

by Claire Edgington

Halloween.
Eerie, Enchanted,
Trick-or-Treating, Frightening, Booing,
Black Cats, Candy Corn, Magic,
Carving, Howling, Pranking,
Frightful, Haunted,
Candy.

Birthdays
by Collin Gerwe

Birthday
Fun, happy,
Laughing, eating, celebrating,
Present, cake, friends,
Partying, aging, honoring
Joyful, exciting,
Birthday!

Ghosts
by Jass Brewer

Ghosts
Mean, evil
Scaring, howling, grueling
Kids, grownups, teenagers
Talking, hiding, fighting
Unhappy, white
Phantom

St. Pius School

by Ryan Arnzen

St. Pius
Fun, Learn,
Teaching, Studying, Laughing
Best School in United States of America
Running, Playing, Teaching,
Great, Large,
School.

Summer

by Claire Edgington and Riley Jordan

No worries in the sun
With my loved one.
We jumped over the waves;
It's all fun and games until we misbehave.
You let me have a head start
Even though you stole my heart.
There were kisses,
There were risks,
Salty air
And sun-kissed hair.
We learned to find
A little peace of mind.
Every summer has a story
Even tho' we didn't get to see Dory.

You Are Perfect

by Grace Martin

Mirror, mirror on the wall,
Who's the fairest one of all?

Why do you care what others think?
As if what they think could make you shrink.

You are perfect just the way you are,
The brightest out of all the stars.

You are you and that's okay;
You are fantastic so do not dismay.

Be Mine Valentine

by Claire Edgington and Riley Jordan

A special day
With my one true love;
As long as you're mine
I'll love you 'til the end of time.

You make me smile from cheek to cheek,
Whenever we walk along this curvy creek.
As you got down on one knee,
I knew it was meant to be.

My heart is perfect because you are inside;
I can't wait to be your beautiful bride.
I picked out the perfect dress,
Remembering the day we both said yes.

You look so fine
When the sun gives you that perfect shine.
Together forever, we'll always be;
I love you just as you love me.

This Mask
by Grace Martin

Don't be fooled by this mask,
For this is a mask of confidence
and a problem-free life.

For this is a mask that
I am afraid to remove,
to show you the real me
Because of what you might think
the unkind words you might say.

I give you the impression
that everything is okay
that I am in control.

But pretending is an art
That is second nature
to me.

Small Fry and Nugget
by Macy Feagan

We were walking down the path
  with the donkeys trotting by
    our sides.
                We, Small Fry, and Nugget
                    came to a complete stop.
                        When we heard the strange noise.
We heard a boom and a crash—
  It was just the goat;
    So we walked along the path at the farm
      With Nugget and Small Fry
        by our sides.

Of the Tigerrrr!

by Luke T

I was waiting in line;
Spotting a dime,
I picked it up
Only to find
A secret hole in the ground
Under the dime.
Of the tigerrrr!

Someone was eating French Toast,
Under the dime of the tigerrrr!
I asked him how he came to be there;
He said, "I did not knowwww
Of the tigerrrr!

Puffy Finger

by Emily Brennen

I was smashed by a tennis racket;
My finger grew puffy.
Puffy finger, puffy finger!
It left a bruise

Puffy finger, puffy finger!
I can't bear to look at it.
EWWW!

Monkeys Like Food

by Annabelle Sunday

Oh monkeys, oh monkeys, oh monkeys like food.

They like fruit,
They'll eat the bugs in your boot.
Monkeys eat bugs, especially slugs.

Oh monkeys, oh monkeys, oh monkeys like food.

Gotta Let Go (a tribute to Grandpa)

by Paige Neuhaus

I was not born yet
But my father told me all about it.
He said, "Your grandpa was a great legacy."
He said, "He joined the army at age sixteen,
And fought for his country;
Lived to be seventy."

When he left, his mother cried
Because she had watched him grow,
but he said to her,
"Some things you just gotta let go".

He married my grandma, Rose.
They stuck together forty-five years.
They loved each other no matter what
Through the laughter and the tears.

She walked down the aisle with a beautiful gown;
Her dad did not want to give her away, but he knew that
Some things you gotta let go.

They had five children including my dad;
They had the smallest house I've ever seen.
With only one bedroom for them all to share.
They ate every night for dinner my grandma's best beans.

When the kids went off to college, Grandpa wanted to tell them,
"No!"
But they all said to him, "Some things you just gotta let go."

Grandpa had six grandkids including me.
He grew very old but nothing could stop him.
He still played with us, even basketball;
He also loved singing church choir hymns.

When he was in the hospital, he was very sick
He still smiled, though.
Before he died, he told us…Some things you gotta let go.

Haiku
by Maddie Maciejewski

My dog is Milo
He is cute and fluffy
I love him so much.

Song
by Grace Martin

This year is going by so fast;
I can't believe how much time has passed.
So many memories I can't replace.
Now it is time to get on with today.
Don't wish your life away
Because there is always today.

Family
by Maddie Maciejewski

My family is the best thing there could ever be;
I love them.
They help me so much;
They are amazing;
My family is important to me.

Beach Days

by Riley Jordan and Claire Edgington

As the sun sets, long past the morning.
It seems like a warning.

The wind in my hair
Oh, the memories we share.

The colors of the sunset blend together;
Why can't I live in this wonderful weather?

Peeking through the great pine
I see the golden outline.

Running through the water with no shoes,
It must be true;

The birds fly
As the dolphins jump into the sky.

Summer Day

Anonymous

Bright, beautiful day,

flowers blooming, birds chirping,

peaceful summer day.

Winter

by Grace Martin

I am counting down the days
Until Christmas Day,
When the children will shout, "Hurray, hurray!"
When people will be united around the globe.

Santa visits the children in his red, silky robe;
Jack Frost comes, sending white, glistening snow.
Christmas carolers will put on a show.

Everyone is smiling so wide;
The day Baby Jesus was born, He became our guide.
He is the Light of the World,
The Savior of our sins.
He will always be, and has always been.

Have a very merry Christmas!
I wish you the best of wishes!

I Wish That I Owned the World

by Jaden Siemer

I wish that I owned the world,

Yeaaaah!

I wish that I owned the world;
I could have whatever I want,
I could do whatever whenever I want
I wish that I owned the world.

Haiku

Snow on the mountains
Lie gratefully in the sun
On a winter day.
by Anonymous

Clouds

by Caroline Citrine

Clouds
All puffy and white
They float in the air;
All puffy and white.
Clouds
All puffy and white.
When you look up in the air
You see them
Clouds
Clouds
Clouds
All puffy and white.

Day after day
A good joke never gets old.
Year after year, things are traditional.
Decade after decade, you hope you never feel older.
Century after century, all things
Like technology
Always advance.

by Ryan Bosch

The Rock

by Brooke Murphy

She called,
she cried,
and died on the inside.

She did not know where to go
so she took a path;
Didn't do the math,
left all she had,
her mom, her dad.

Her friends were mad;
She dumped, she jumped
From friend to friend; left the one
Who used to lend.

She had Green;
that was it.
She tried to hold him,
But he ran away.

His ghost still lay,
waiting for the day
she came back.

She left with the snake
That took her to a lake
Where people can't come out
Until they take a great fall.

Green and her rock waited;
Waited a great long time,
But she was too busy drowning
To see it true.

Her friends became blue;
Green got tired and left.
The rock stayed still.

Luke,
Creative, Fun, Happy,
Ryan T.
Kendama, Paintball, Golf,
Bored, Excited, Happy,
Money, Macbook Pro, My own room,
Pencils, Help, Paper,
Death, Tornadoes, Homework,
Niagra Falls,
Human,
Edgewood, Kentucky
T.

Collin
Who is smart, kind, and blonde,
Who is the brother of Max and Ava,
Who loves soccer, Xbox, and Kings Island,
Who feels good, happy, and energetic,
Who needs food, drinks, and video games,
Who gives compliments, help, and happiness,
Who fears bears, Slenderman, and getting bad grades,
Who would like to see the pyramids of Egypt,
Who wishes he had a tree house,
Who is helpful,
Who is a resident of Erlanger,
Gerwe.

Jaden

Who is awesome, cool, fun
Who is the brother of Rachel, Tara, Marisa, Logan, and Stefan,
Who loves summer, winter, and Hilton Head Island
Who feels happy, excited, and nice;

Who needs a house, food, and water
Who gives happiness, gifts, and food;

Who fears death, being poor, and car crashes
Who would like to see the Caribbean, Arizona, and a Miami Marlins baseball game
Who wishes he owned a major league baseball team;

Who is funny
Who is a resident of Edgewood

Siemer.

Claire

Who is smart, kind, and athletic
Who is the sister of Andrew and Alex
Who loves her family, the beach, and summer
Who feels blessed, happy, and loved
Who needs her family, friends, and lots of love
Who gives happiness, hugs, and smiles
Who fears birds, spiders, and sharks
Who would like to see Rome
Who wishes for everlasting life
Who is always smiling
Who is a resident of Edgewood,
Edgington

Emily
Who is brave, funny, and athletic
Who is the sister of Sarah
Who loves summer, Lulu, and soccer
Who feels happy, energetic, and excited
Who needs love, kindness, and laughter
Who fears haunted houses, spiders, and clowns
Who would like to see the Eiffel Tower
Who is nice
Who is a resident of Erlanger
Brennen

Brooke
Who is adventurous, sassy, and preppy
Who is the sister of Britton and Brynn
Who loves volleyball, Lily Pulitzer, and Clipper
Who feels happy, crazy, and excited
Who needs friends, blueberry muffins, and music
Who gives smiles, happiness, and joy
Who fears homework, math, and pistachios
Who would like to see Andy win the Sweet Sixteen Tournament
Who is a star
Who is a resident of Prestwicke
Murphy.

Paige
Who is creative, smart, and talented
Who is the sister of Emma, Tara, and Rachel
Who loves art, puppies, and Lily Pulitzer
Who feels unique, happy, and stressed
Who needs a dog, her mom to fix her curtain, and a vacation
Who gives her time, effort, and work to school
Who fears roller coasters, being stuck in a big crowd, and tornadoes
Who would like to see Palm Beach, Memphis, and Alabama
Who wishes to see her grandpa
Who is unique
Who is a resident of Kentucky
Neuhaus

Ryan
Who is an active, tall, healthy baseball player
Who is the brother of Tommy and Mandy
Who loves baseball, his pets, and his family
Who needs food, water, and shelter
Who gives time, money, and food
Who fears snakes, heights, and sharks
Who wants to see an All-Star game
And London and New York
Who wishes everything were free
Who is a resident of his parents' house
Arnzen

Aria
Who is courageous, creative, and talented
Who is the sister of Ryan
Who loves volleyball, shopping, and dogs
Who feels happy
Who needs a pet dog
Who gives cookies, chocolate, and brownies
Who fears snakes, sharks, and clowns,
Who would like to see Newsies
Who wishes for the best car ever
Who is courageous, creative, and talented
Who is a resident of Edgewood
Meier

Ezzy
Who is smart, athletic, and kind
Who is funny and tall
Who is the brother of Sommer
Who loves Florida, Gatlinburg, and Elk Lake
Who loves basketball and baseball
Who needs friends, family, and pets
Who gives joy, happiness, and love
Who fears spiders, lions, and bears
Who would like to see the Bahamas
Who is a resident of Edgewood
Shields

Ryan

Who is athletic, fast, and smart
Who is the brother of Anthony and Christine

Who loves America, Italy, and Germany
Who loves drawing, summer, his dog and cats, and Manhunt

Who feels pain, fear, and excitement
Who needs fun, care, and attention
Who gives care, attention, and fun

Who fears early death, Teletubbies, and sharks
Who would like to play Hide-and-Seek at night in a corn maze

Who wishes and hopes for the best
Who is a fast runner
Who is a resident of Edgewood

Bosch

Corey

Who is a killer snowboarder

Who is a brother of Chase, Ava, and Skyler

Who loves Hawaii, skateboarding, and Lacrosse

Who feels happy, sad, and mad

Who needs a trillion dollars, pizza, and the coolest shoes

Who gives time to others, accompanies others, gives money to the poor

Who fears death, school, and scuffing his new shoes

Who would like to see T-Wayne

Who wants unlimited wishes

Who is a resident of Kruer Court

Dudderar

Elliot

Who is big, nice, and smart

Who is the brother of Britney, Max, Lincoln, Oliver, Dexter, Faith, and Gus

Who loves fall, football, and Larosa's

Who feels stressed out during school, happy during fall, and mad

When it is Sunday night and I have to go to bed early

Who needs more sleep, more food, and more summer

Who gives friendship, happiness, and fun

Who fears murderers, serial killers, and psychos

Who would like to see Ireland

Who wishes he could fly

Who is a nice and funny friend

Who is a resident of Covington

Bent

Grace

Who is athletic, smart, funny
Who is the sister of Joe

Who loves autumn, dogs, and volleyball
Who feels happy when she goes to Kohl's
Who feels excited when she is with her friends

Who needs to have fun, be with her family, and go to college
Who gives smiles, laughs, and compliments

Who fears dolls, clowns, and sharks
Who would like to see her great-grandma Grace
Who wishes for child abuse to end

Who is witty
Who is a resident of Edgewood
Martin

Ethan

Who is funny, likes sports, and has many friends
Who is a brother of Brandon
Who loves pasta with Alfredo sauce and meatballs,
Who feels happy most of the time
Who needs food, water, friends, and family
Who gives his friends happiness
Who fears snakes
Who would like to see Europe
Who would run 13.1 miles
Who wishes he could have a time machine
Who is nice most all the time
Who is a resident of Erlanger

Wever

Macy

Who is funny, adventurous, dramatic
Who is the sister of Isabella
Who loves Netflix and nature

Who feels inspired, happy, blessed
Who needs friends, family, love, and a genie
Who gives hope, inspiration, laughs
Who fears spiders, clowns, Fefe

Who would like to see world peace
and Greece
Who wishes to have a family one day

Who is nice, funny, hopeful, blessed, wishful
Who is a resident of Edgewood

Feagan

Quickly the ball was thrown through the air
Chasing-- the ball continues to fly past
Softly the ball hits the ground
Bouncing the ball continues onward
Loudly the crowd cheers
Running the runner smiles
Quickly the runner is home
Cheering! The team won!

by Annabelle Sunday

Slowly the pitcher reaches the mound
Watching closely for a sign
Throwing the ball as fast as he can
Waiting for the batter to strike.

Mightily the batter makes contact
Running the bases, he slows at third
Then speeding ahead,
He makes it home for the win.

by Ryan Arnzen

November

Anonymous

The reds, oranges, and yellow
Of leaves falling to the ground.
I love the crisp, red apples
So juicy and round.

It is becoming cold outside;
I can feel the brisk breeze.
The grass is no longer green and plush;
All the leaves are gone from the trees.

The days are becoming shorter;
Soon I will see frost in the early morning.
It is time to wear jackets and gloves;
And for the dead flowers, I will be mourning.

I look forward to Thanksgiving Day,
Turkey and corn with pumpkin pie.
I will be surrounded by my family;
The November air will be dry.

Soon to come…
The white snowflakes, fluttering to the ground;
The longer nights and shorter days;
Animals fattening up
To hibernate, leave, or stay.

Chapter Five:
Homeroom 702

Drew
Who is smart, kind, and fun
Who is the brother of Seth, Marisa, Mia, Kira, and Alex
Who loves winter, family, and soccer
Who feels friendly, curious, and happy
Who needs family, friends, and water
Who gives time, effort, and respect
Who fears choking, being stranded, and needles
Who would like to see the Grand Canyon
Who wishes he could fly
Who is small
Who is a resident of Edgewood
Kent

Anne-Marie
Who is kind, happy, and thoughtful
Who is the sister of Kassi, Whitnie, and Ella
Who love going outside, weekends, and people
Who feels happy, energetic, and confused all the time
Who needs happiness, hope, and fun
Who fears murderers, Cincinnati at night, and no Wi-Fi
Who would like to see Portugal
Who wishes life was easier
Who is honest
Who is a resident of Constitution
Wright

Kade
Who is smart, fun, and nice
Who is the brother of Teagan, Tate, and Jace
Who loves Montana, fishing, and sports
Who feels happy, friendly, and bold
Who needs family, friends, and food
Who gives time, heart, and effort
Who fears being stranded in the ocean, Great White sharks, and choking
Who would like to see a grizzly bear, Los Angeles, and Mt. Everest
Who wishes to fly
Who is a resident of the U.S.A.
Kruer

Jackson
Who is funny, friendly, and sincere
Who is the brother of Matt and Helena
Who loves Moose, his dog, soccer, and recess
Who feels great, fresh, and awesome,
Who needs an X-Box, Forza Horizon, and two new golf clubs
Who gives hope, laughter, and fun
Who fears spiders, cliffs, and scary movies
Who would like to see Jamaica
Who wishes he owned a 1978 Corvette Stingray
Who is a resident of Edgewood
Frisch

Lauren
Who is kind, smart, and athletic
Who is the sister of Mitchell and Kate
Who loves soccer, fall, and art
Who feels happy, peaceful, and relaxed
Who needs patience, family and friends
Who gives time, talent, and kindness
Who would like to see Italy
Who wishes for a pet
Who is caring
Who is a resident of Erlanger

Davey

Isabelle
Who is funny, nice, intelligent
Who is the sister of Henry and Grace
Who loves fall, winter, and summer
Who feels hungry, tired, and energetic
Who needs food, water, and her dog
Who gives time to the community—
Help to those in need
Who fears drowning, spiders, and sharks
Who would like to see Australia
Who wishes she were a billionaire
Who is a resident of Edgewood

Bennett

Hope

Who is athletic, funny, and kind.
Who is the sister of Adam.
Who loves to run, play basketball, and go to Florida.
Who feels happy, sometimes sad, and sometimes excited.
Who needs food, family, and friends
Who gives hugs, good advice, and good friendship.
Who fears snakes, dying, and cracking her phone.
Who would like to see the Bengals win the Super Bowl.
Who wishes to get into a good college.
Who wishes that she can get straight A's this year.
Who is a resident of Edgewood.

McNickle

Ava

Who is fun, nice, and humorous
Who is a sister of Devin

Who loves fall, soccer, and baked potatoes
Who feels happy when she gets ice cream
and when she wins a soccer game

Who needs money, fun, happiness
Who gives food, laughter, fun

Who fears when there is no Wi-Fi
And going into space and kidnappers

Who would like to see New Orleans
Who wishes to get a kitten

Who is resident of Edgewood

Hassan

Reece

Who is nice, athletic, funny, energetic, and charming
Who is the brother of Cameron, Jay, and Chelsea
Who loves sports, family, friends, and money
Who feels sad when his mom says no Hyper Walk
Who is happy with friends and when playing basketball and football
Who needs a Hyper Walk, Retro 11s and Retro 4s
Who gives himself food, high fives, and candy on the fourth of July
Who fears failing, honey badgers, and bad people
Who would like to see Rae Sremmurd at Riverbend
Who wishes to achieve greatness
Who is a resident of Edgewood

Murphy

Liam

Who is nice, funny, good-looking, and cool
Who is the brother of Ava Gray
Who loves spring, winter, and summer
Who feels great all the time
Who needs water, food, clothing
Who gives help and makes happy
Who fears bad people, snakes, homework
Who would like to see Jamaica, and skydive, and roller coaster
Who is nice, funny, chill
Who is a resident of Edgewood

Gray

Ashton
Who is athletic, funny
Who is the brother of Morgan and Lily
Who loves to play baseball and basketball
Who feels happy, excited, and sad sometimes
Who needs sports, fun, and friends
Who gives money, fun, and time
Who fears snakes, sharks, and poisonous stuff
Who would like to see the World Series
Who wishes he had all the money in the world
Who is happy
Who is a resident of Erlanger
Isler

Claire
Who is unique, friendly, and loud
Who is the sister of Jack, Beck, and Chloe
Who loves tea, music, and art
Who feels unique, happy, and loved
Who gives hope, entertainment, and good vibes
Who fears being unwanted, losing hope, and not being herself
Who would like to see New York City, again
Who wishes to be free
Who is bold
Who is a resident of the U.S.A.
Dunham

Jason
Who is funny, friendly, smart
Who is the brother of Jared and Rachel
Who loves golf, magic, and quizzes
Who feels happy when others have good fortune
Who feels sad when he plays a bad round of golf
Who is cold during winter
Who needs another dog to calm down, get some sleep
Who fears super heights, scary movies, bears
Who would like to see a Jamaican penguin with dreadlocks,
wearing a red, yellow, and green hat
Who wishes he had unlimited time to golf
Who is a resident of Kentucky

Reid

Chris
Who is funny and smart
Who is the brother of JP, Lincoln, Elizabeth, Max, and Anastasia
Who loves soccer, games, and jokes
Who feels happy, sad, mad
Who gives friendship, happiness, and ideas
Who fears sharks, snakes, and drowning
Who would like to see Rome
Who wishes that he had unlimited money
Who is a resident of Lexington Drive

Mason

Olivia

Who is nice, organized, athletic, and smart
Who is the sister of Claire and Meredith
Who loves cross country, soccer, and winter
Who feels happy, relaxed, and calm
Who needs patience, friends, and family
Who gives talent, kindness, and happiness
Who fears spiders, wasps, and snakes
Who would like to see Dubai
Who wishes for a horse
Who is a perfectionist
Who is a resident of Edgewood

Maschinot

Abby

Who is tall, funny, athletic
Who is the sister of Noah
Who loves volleyball, the beach, and dogs
Who feels sometimes happy, sad, and excited
Who needs family, friends, and food
Who gives great piggyback rides, hugs, and pep talks
Who fears spiders, the end of the world, and when there is no Wi Fi,
Who would like to see space,
Who wishes to make the Olympics,
Who is a resident of Edgewood,

Powers

Matt
Who is nice, funny, and athletic
Who is the brother of Mike and Jacob
Who loves summer, family, and sports
Who feels caring, kind, and confident
Who needs respect, kindness, and care
Who gives effort, support, and love
Who fears giant bombs and snakes
Who wishes to play in the NFL
Who is skillful
Who is a resident of Edgewood
Henn

Jordan
Who is funny and nice
Who is the sister of Delaney
Who loves her cat, the pool, and volleyball
Who feels happy, tired, hungry
Who needs food, water, and her cat
Who gives time, food, money
Who fears heights, horror movies, and sharks
Who would like to see California
Who wishes to have a dog
Who is a resident of Edgewood
Gillum

Happy, peaceful day,
Having fun in the sun,
Blue skies, flowers blooming
Summer has just begun.
It is a beautiful day,
And everything is going my way.

by Lauren Davey

Slowly the golfer stepped up to the tee,
silencing the crowd.

Suddenly, the world was still,
waiting for the golfer to swing.

Quickly, the golfer swung,
crushing the ball towards the green.

Amazingly, the ball went into the hole,
Urging the crowd to go wild.

by Jason Reid

Literally, my life is
volleyball every single night
messy hair and hard spikes
literally my life.

by Abby Powers

Clouds
by Claire Dunham

I am somewhat like the clouds in the sky
sitting unnoticed and still
But one day I appear
darker, with more purpose
And as you fly up
my water drizzles down
drowning the thoughts
until they are submerged
Still no one dares to say a word.

Just a Galaxy Away
by Claire Dunham

Last night I dreamed in a galaxy
and ran around the world
as the stars sang in my ears.
I jumped over Jupiter
and swam on Mars
laughing with the constellations
as the stardust fell on my face
like glistening rain.

City love
why do you do this
city love
you are too much
your eyes like headlights
coming for me
Oh city love, set me free.

You are my joy
you are my pain
I have feelings inside
but, you don't know
inside.

You are my fire
you are my match
how long will this burning last?
You know we will fade to gray
why don't you leave today?

by Claire Dunham

Don't just sit there, you've got to get to work
You have to get
busyyy, busyyy, busyyy, busyyy.

Walked on to the busy streets of New York,
Lights shining all on me.
Taxi cabs and cars all in a row,
Honking, honking, honking at me.

by Olivia Maschinot

Fefe the Cat
By Jordan Gillum

As I walked in the room
And saw him standing there
    I couldn't help but watch and stare
        As he hit the quan, dabbing and whipping,
           I looked at him and said, "Hey! Are you tripping?"
           He saw me staring at him and knew he wasn't going to stay
           So he got up and Nae Naed away.

Jason's Song

by Jason Reid

Hellllooooooo I am Jason
I kinda like bacon
But what really hits the spot
is Mountain Dew and a candy named Zots.

I am good at golf and kendama
I like alpacas but I don't like llamas
I really like buffalo wings
When they're baking in the oven
I wait 'til it dings.

I am good at playing video games
But trust that is not my ticket to fame
My sponsor for golf is Srixon
And did I mention
I'm pretty great at rapping
But I'm not good at clapping
And sometimes I sing songs
I am also pretty dang great at ping pong.

What I Found in My Locker

by Lauren Davey

Books scattered all around,
a crayon waiting to be found,
a toy car that does not move,
a Hawaiian girl that likes to groove,
an old snack that weighs an ounce,
a soccer ball that does not bounce,
a pencil that does not write,
a picture of a starry night,
a cute little pencil bag,
                  a locker shelf
                      starting
                        to
                          sag.
This is my biggest fear,
Cleaning out my locker this year!

What I Found in My Locker

by Olivia Maschinot

Papers all crumbled high to low,
  a pencil that was supposed to glow,
    artsy pictures on the wall,
      every day they would fall
        old snacks that have turned brown,
    books scattered all around,
   a small soccer ball,
  a bunch of bugs on the wall,
    a soccer uniform that's very stinky,
      also a yummy, yummy Twinkie,
  a kendama (I'm not so good at),
   a toy dog who is really fat.

Quickly, the swimmers get ready
  Laughing with friends.
Quietly, the swimmers step on the block
Buzzing, the buzzer alerts the swimmers,
Swiftly, each swims against the others,
  Trying to be the first.
  Swimming, swimming
  That last one was me.

by Ava Hassan

  Slowly, the ball rolled
  Making its way to the goal.
  Skillfully, the goalie dived
  Trying to stop the ball.
  Finally, the ball crossed the line
    igniting the crowd.
  Quickly, the fans ran onto the field
Lifting the star player onto their shoulders.

by Drew Kent

Soccer

by Jackson Frisch

Fun, athletic,
Exciting, tiring, amazing,
NKSA, Peewee Football field,
Mary Queen of Heaven
Communicating, positioning, scoring,
International, competitive,
L. Messi

Breadsticks

by Jason Reid

Breasticks
Long, tan
Eating, Nibbling, Swallowing
Butter, Salt, Yeast
Baking, Mixing, Pounding
Amazing, Tasty
Wheat

Fear Fest
by Hope McNickle

King's Island
Spooky, Funny
Screaming, Crying, Running
Clowns, Blood, Pigs
Terrifying, Scaring, Sliding
Crazy, Exciting
Fear Fest!

Hamster
cute, happy
chewing, running, climbing
animal, creature, pet
jumping, walking, sleeping
nocturnal, awesome
mammal

by Calista Solo

Soccer
Fun, Competitive
Shooting, Running, Passing
Players, Rivals, Goalie
Panting, Throwing, Kicking
Exciting, Amazing
Game

by Olivia Maschinot

French Fries

by Reece Murphy

Fries
French, Golden
Ordering, Chewing, Swallowing
Tomatoes, Salt, Side
Paying, Smashing, Savoring
Tasty, Curly
Fries

Alaska
cold, barren
howling, growling, whirling
bear, wolf, fish
hunting, fishing, boating
natural, beautiful
Alaska

by Chris Mason

Football
by Matt Henn

Football
scary, big
running, hitting, moving
NFL, college, high school
kicking, intercepting, throwing
amazing, awesome
sports.

Bengals,
Tough, undefeated
Running, kicking, throwing
Pac-Man, AJ, Dalton
Tackling, intercepting
Catching
Amazing, 8-0
Footballers.

by Kade Kruer

Baseball
Fun, awesome
Hitting, throwing, catching
Ballpark, dugout, water
Sliding, leaping, diving
Athletic, exercise
Sport.

by Zach Tucker

Volleyball
Upbeat, exciting
Yelling, passing, strategizing
Hitters, libero, setters
Hitting, diving, setting
Teamwork, competitive
Sport

by Abby Powers

New York
Big, Busy
Honking, Running, Yelling
Businesses, People, Buildings
Seeing, Shopping, Eating
Crowded, Beautiful
The Big Apple.

by Andrew Bosch

Olive Garden

by Ava Hassan

Italian, yummy
baking, eating, cooking
food, pasta, breadsticks
making, tasting, taking
amazing, loud
calories.

Halloween

by Drew Kent

Halloween

Spooky, creepy

Screaming, scaring, terrifying

Monsters, ghosts, ghouls,

Yelling, shouting, running

Scary, slimy

Day of the Dead.

Ghost

Spooky, scary

Flying, hovering, scaring

Haunted house, Jasper

Terrifying, shrieking, creeping

White, fearful

Halloween.

by Ashton Isler

Creature Encounter

by Isabelle Bennett

As I walk through the dense and humid forest,

the heat beats on my shoulders.

I hear a noise creeping behind me.

I turn; there is nothing there.

The leaves rustle.

I turn again and see it.

The dark, beady eyes stare at me.

My instinct is to run.

I think better of that

Because I know

I will be chased.

My heart is racing,

My breathing quick;

I know it will attack.

But just as I believe

that I am doomed,

the black bear runs away.

Fiercely, the players take the field,
speeding as they move with style.
Desperately, she tries for one more.
Kicking powerfully, she misses.
Luckily, she is fouled.
Breathing the cold air, she sets up.
Nervously, she kicks and
SHE SCORES!
Screaming, the crowd erupts!

by Isabelle Bennett

Holocaust

by Jacob Danneman

Holocaust:
Smoke fills the sky,
With many children's cries.
Countless persons have died,
Beneath the dark sky
With many souls that are dry.
Why could the sky **not** cry
With children and parents saying goodbye,
With smoke still drifting through the sky?

Apple yum apple
Red yellow and green apples
Apples are yummy

```
                    s
                    t
                    e
      apple apple   m   apple apple
       apple apple apple apple  apple apple
      yum apple yum yum apple apple yum apple
      red yellow green red yellow green apples yum
      crunchy juicy crunchy juicy crunchy juicy crunchy
      delicious delicious    tasty    delicious delicious
      apple   apple  apple apple apple apple  apple  apple
      apple   apple  apple apple apple apple  apple   apple
      yum yum  yum  yum  yum yum yum yum yum yum
        yum yum yum yum yum yum yum yum yum yum
         red yellow green red yellow green red yellow
         crunchy crunchy crunchy crunchy crunchy
          juicy juicy juicy juicy juicy juicy juicy
             apple apple      apple apple
              apple              apple
```

Chapter Six:

Homeroom 703

Jenna

Who is nice, smart, and fun
Who is the sister of Maria, Drew, Jacob, Caroline, and Johnny
Who loves to shop, play volleyball, and do theater
Who feels happy when getting a good grade, sad when I watch sad movies,
excited when I get to go to King's Island

Who needs a good education, family, friends
Who gives time to others, love to family, good effort to teachers
Who fears spiders, ghosts, and the snake pit
Who would like to see Rome
Who wishes to end world hunger

Who is cool, clever, and creative
Who is a resident of the Bluegrass State

Danneman

Logan

Who is kind, smart, funny, and happy
Who is the brother of Thomas and Mason
Who loves sports, animals, thunder, roller coasters, and Fifa
Who feels happy, lucky, and blessed
Who needs food, water, and shelter
Who gives happiness, kindness, and help
Who fears sharks, demons, and falling off a cliff
Who would like to see Dubai
Who wishes for one million dollars
Who is a resident of Independence

Finke

Trey

Who is brave, kind, and adorable

Who is the brother of Annie and Jackson

Who loves soccer, fishing, and going on vacations

Who feels changes, happiness, and sadness
Who needs food, water, shelter, and God

Who gives his humor, joyfulness, and kindness to others

Who fears nothing

Who would like to see Barca play, South Africa (again), the World Cup, and Dubai
Who wishes to play on the King's Hammer Red Team

Who is charming

Who is a resident of Crestview Hills

Gronotte

Kierstin

Who is kind, friendly, and unique

Who has two step-brothers and a step-sister

Who loves animals, summer, and winter

Who feels happy, joyful, faithful

Who needs family, friends, and love

Who gives her time, money for birthdays, and gifts

Who fears being homeless, bridges collapsing, and snakes

Who would like to see Italy

Who wishes to have another dog

Who is courageous

Who is a resident of Erlanger

Haas

Skyllar

Who is nice, energetic, and hard-working
Who is the sister of Stella
Who loves her family, sports, pets
Who feels happiness, loved, and important
Who needs food, water, and shelter
Who gives time, effort, and energy
Who fears birds, bridges, and not having a job when she grows up
Who would like to go to Hawaii
Who wishes to do well in school
Who is understanding
Who is a resident of Edgewood

Jacocks

J.J.

Who is smart, hard-working, and curious
Who is the brother of Bella and Luka
Who loves his family, guitar, and tennis
Who feels supported, happy, and thankful
Who needs food, water, and something to do
Who gives his time, effort, and advice
Who fears the devil, plane crashes, and falling
Who is motivated, creative, and independent
Who is a resident of Crescent Springs

Kampinga

Corinne

Who is athletic, smart, and thoughtful
Who is the sister of Tyler and Drew
Who loves sports, family, and friends
Who feels happy, blessed, and important
Who needs patience, more time, and less homework
Who gives advice, effort, and love
Who fears failure, spiders, and CLOWNS
Who would like to see the British Virgin Islands
Who wishes for world peace
Who is a leader
Who is a resident of Edgewood

Laws

Tre

Who is awesome, cool, and independent
Who is the sibling of no one
Who loves Wengen, Switzerland, his dog Piper, and his family
Who feels pain, joy, and happiness
Who needs food, water, and oxygen

Who gives money, help, and friendship
Who fears nothing, no one, and nowhere
Who would like to see Australia
Who wishes for world peace

Who is smart
Who is a resident of the United States of America

Lohre

Ross
Who is funny and smart
Who is the brother of Lydia
Who loves KFC, soccer, and Cocoa, his dog
Who feels smart, tired, and happy
Who needs another dog, a Segway, and caring
Who gives happiness, service, and kindness
Who fears ghosts, UFOs, and spiders
Who would like to see a pink lake in Australia
Who wishes he would grow up to play soccer
Who is an amazing soccer player
Who is a resident of Erlanger
Lux

Grant
Who is nice, fun, athletic
Who is the brother of Nate and Olivia
Who loves soccer, basketball, and other sports
Who feels happy; mad when my brother annoys me
Who needs food, water, and family
Who gives thanks, joy, and happiness
Who fears clowns, horror movies, caterpillars
Who would like to see the World Cup
Who wishes he could fly
Who is a resident of Edgewood
Montelisciani

Sky
Who is kind, fun, and happy
Who is the sister of Anna
Who loves family, friends, and animals
Who feels happy, blessed, and loved
Who needs Jesus, family, and friends
Who gives time, love, and effort
Who fears heights and being poor
Who would like to see Paris
Who is FUN!
Who is a resident of Independence
Morris

Ava
Who is outgoing, funny, and nice
Who is the sister of Lauren, Alex, Will, and Owen
Who loves Hawaii, soccer, and summer
Who feels loved, happy, perfect
Who needs food, water, and family
Who gives love, time, help
Who fears spiders, snakes, and the end of the world
Who would like to see everyone happy
Who wishes to end world hunger
Who is a resident of Edgewood and Florence
Quigley

Jacob
Who is smart, funny, kind
Who is the brother of no one
Who loves baseball, summer, and vacation
Who feels happy, excited, good
Who needs an I-pad, food, clothes
Who gives care, love, kindness
Who fears heights, roller coasters, and moving away
Who would like to see the World Series
Who wishes for Reds season tickets
Who is a resident of Edgewood
Robke

Brayden
Who is friendly, funny, and truthful
Who is the brother of Logan
Who loves soccer, volleyball, and Disney
Who feels happy and energetic, and tired sometimes
Who needs food, water, and family
Who gives time, food, and dedication
Who fears snakes, nothing else, and nobody
Who wishes to have a lot of money
Who is kind
Who is a resident of Erlanger
Sanning

Lily
Who is nice, smart, funny
Who is the sister of Clare
Who loves her family, her house, and her dog
Who feels happy, excited, and important
Who needs cookies, clothes, and Starbucks
Who gives money, time, and gifts
Who fears bugs, monsters, and robbers
Who would like to see Hawaii
Who wishes to have a good life when she is older
Who is good at dance
Who is a resident of Edgewood
Shay

Ava
Who is nice, friendly, fun
Who is the sister of Nolan, Jack, Grace
Who loves Netflix, and to play sports and shop
Who feels important, good, happy
Who needs family, friends, shelter
Who gives love, joy, effort
Who fears the devil, a snake pit, and spiders
Who would like to see the Bahamas
Who wishes for EVERYTHING!
Who is a resident of the Shields family home
Shields

Jared
Who is smart, fun, cool
Who is the brother of John, Jordan, Jason
Who loves sports, traveling, and riding his quad
Who feels smart, loved, athletic
Who needs food, water, shelter
Who gives presents and care to the poor
Who fears monsters, spiders, snakes
Who would like to hike the Grand Canyon and raft out
Who wishes he had more money
Who is a resident of his house
Simon

Maggie
Who is kind, smart, and athletic
Who is the sister of Riley and J.D.
Who loves sports, family, and friends
Who feels happy, loved, and important
Who needs food, water, and shelter
Who gives kindness, happiness, and effort
Who fears snakes, bridges, and spiders
Who would like to see the World Cup
Who wishes for world peace
Who is a friend
Who is a resident of Edgewood
Smith

Riley
Who is athletic, small, and nice
Who is the sister of Gage, Keith, Tori
Who loves her hamster, family, and sports
Who feels loved, cared for, joyful, and happy
Who needs food, clothing, shelter, warmth, and water
Who gives happiness, love, joy, faith, and courage
Who fears high places and falling bridges
Who would like to see the White House
Who wishes for her own puppy or kitten
Who is a resident of her parents' home

Morgan

Josh
Who is the best of all
Who is the brother of Matthew, Mike, Katie, Chloe, and Luke
Who loves Florida, Texas, Kentucky, Florida State, and the Texas Longhorns
Who feels happy, tired, and joyful
Who needs a Motovox, Skywalker
Who gives money to friends
Who fears getting poked in the eye
Who wishes to control things with his mind
Who has the peaceful, easy feeling
Who is a resident of Crestview Hills

Summe

Michael

Who is fun, kind, preppy
Who is the brother to Johnny and Matthew
Who loves winter, soccer, and New York
Who feels happy, loved, smiley
Who needs Netflix, Starbucks, Vineyard Vines
Who gives presents, happiness, gifts
Who fears heights, robbers, monsters,
Who would like to see all the Disney Parks
Who wishes to live happily ever after
Who is a resident of Crestview Hills

Thiel

Ella

Who is smart, creative, talented, fun, and interesting
Who is the sister of Claire, Gabe, and June
Who loves fall, and to bake and sleep in
Who feels happy, smart, and loved
Who needs to learn new things
Who gives time, talent, and cookies
Who fears not reaching goals, not doing something right, and missing out
Who would like to see Europe
Who wishes she had her own room
Who is a resident of Edgewood

Weaver

Zach
Who is fast, strong, and athletic
Who is the brother of Sam and Allie
Who loves sports
Who feels happy, sad, and mad
Who needs food, water, and school
Who gives happiness, thanks, and joy
Who fears haunted houses, centipedes, and snakes
Who would like to see Paris
Who wishes for a dirt bike
Who is a resident of the Weidinger home
Weidinger

Heavily, the snow falls, covering the ground.
Tweeting, the birds sing, filling the forest with songs.
Laughing, the children run for their sleds.
Quickly, they race down the hill.
Cheering, they steer their way on the steep path.
Stomping in the snow, they find refuge inside.
Cozily, the fire crackles, giving warmth.
Happily, everyone sips hot chocolate.
Tip-toeing to their beds,
the children seek a long winter's nap.

Anonymous

Rapidly, the ball is dribbled down the field,
looking for the open pass.
Hesitating, the striker takes a shot;
Slowly, the ball heads toward the goal.
Cheering loudly, the fans yell
as we win the game!

by Sky Morris

Carefully, the ball bounced,

touching the gym floor.

Gently, the ball was lifted,

finding the player's hands.

Confidently, the ball was tossed

spinning in the air.

Powerfully, the ball was hit,

flying away from her grasp.

by Ella Weaver

Gracefully, I dance across the stage,
leaping high.

Daintily, I run to my place.
Running, I move swiftly.

Quietly, the backdrop changes.
Spinning, I twirl.

Humbly, I bow.
Gracefully, I leave the stage.

by Lily Shay

Swiftly, the dancer glides across the floor,
pointing her toes in an arc.
Slowly, she lifts her legs high in the air,
landing in a graceful pose.
Beautifully, she smiles at the audience,
elevating her arms.
Elegantly, she curtsies
for all to see.

by Jenna Danneman

Swiftly, the ball was kicked,
finding the top corner.
Quickly, the goalie dived;
Amazingly, he saved it.
Slowly, the ball came rolling back
to the striker.

by Trey Gronotte

Stood out in the rain,
let it soak me down
before I called you.
I called to you;
didn't see me there.

by Jared Simon

Quietly, the birds chirp in the distance,
singing songs of nature.
Gently, the stream flows,
teeming with graceful fish.
Slowly, the sun rises.
A small child watches
from his window,
Motionlessly staring at the beauty,
longing to be
where the stream flows
and the fish swim.

by Corinne Laws

Nature
Beautiful, Free
Chirping, Flourishing, Blooming
Growing, Living, Glistening
Refreshing, Vibrant
Outdoors

by Corinne Laws

Haiku
Ella Weaver

The rain was falling.
The warm sun was rising;
What a wonderful sight!

Oh, Florida!
by Josh Summe

Oh, Florida!
I love you!
You are warm.
I love you!
You are sand.
I love you!
You are ocean.
I love you!
You are sunny
YEAH!

Fall
Crisp, breezy
Baking, falling, learning
Leaves, pie, family
Raking, eating, playing
Cool, fresh
Autumn.

by Ella Weaver

November
Fall, autumn
November.
Chilly, fires
November.
Leaves are falling
Oh, November.
Chilly, boots
November.

by Maggie Smith

Halloween
Spooky, Creepy
Terrifying, Spooking, Costuming
Ghosts, Goblins, Witches
Brewing, Ewing, Gooing
Slimy, Sticky
October 31

by Michael Thiel

Halloween
by Jenna Danneman

Scary, horrifying
running, jumping, scaring
costumes, candy, cobwebs
laughing, screaming, haunting
dark, frightening
monsters.

Halloween Town
by Ava Shields

Evil, Spooking
Brewing, Scaring, Turning
Witches, Vampires, Skeletons
Flying, Laughing, Moaning
Icky, Creepy
Movie

Christmas
Merry, Bright
Snowing, Sledding, Singing
Santa, Cookies, Snow
Loving, Caring, Snuggling
Warm, Cozy
Noel.

by Sky Morris

Merry almost Christmas X3.
Open your presents and eat some cake
Because it's coming very soon, soooo
Merry almost Christmas X2.
Eat some cookies right away.
It is coming very soon, soooo
Merry almost Christmas X2.
Get your tree.
Merry almost Christmas X3

by Brayden Sanning

Christmas
excitement, coziness
laughing, loving, celebrating
Santa, Grinch, elf
caroling, sledding, baking
holly, jolly
December 25

by Ava Quigley

My Buddy, Popcorn
by Riley Morgan

As sweet as a buttercup
As salty as the sea
As tiny as a pea
He pops his little head
And hisses at me.
Buddy, give me a chance.
I've had other hamsters,
But they are not quite
As special as you.
So I ask you, please,
PLEASE like me.

                You and me
           In the land of the free
           We had a good time
             A very fine time.
             Land of the free—
              It is my home,
           The home that I love.
                    by Ava Quigley

Oh, and it's all because I walk, walk, walk
Into the woodlands,
And I walk, walk, walk
Along the stream.
And when the stars come out at night,
I just sit tight.

I gaze up into the sky,
Hear my brother's whisper,
Among the sounds of night.
Why would I ever want to go?

I can see the mountains
When I am here.
Why, why would I ever
Want to leave this world
Of mine?

Someone asked me:
Did I know the world had changed?

by J.J. Kampinga

The Look
by Sky Morris

Through the cold winter night,
I feel something looking at me,
Not a look of hatred,
Not a loving look,
Just a cold stare.

I hear steps through the woods,
Though not heavy ones;
Light ones.
Out of the corner of my eye,
I see bright blue eyes,
and a heavy coat of gray.
It springs out
Of the woods.

To my surprise,
The wolf walks along side me.
Quietly, our feet pitter-patter
Along the rough woodland floor.

The crystal eyes look at me;
I look back.
We both freeze
In silence
As we gaze into each other's eyes.

My breath is heavy under the cold winter air;
The wind blows stronger;
I wish to be home.

My feet get lighter, my heart slower.
I wander through the dark
In search of sleep.

The wolf and I walk
To a large dugout.
She cannot speak
But she tells me,
"Go in,
To my den."

Inside, there is
A small leaf pile
For me to lay down my head.
My eyes grow heavy;
I drift into sleep.

When I awake,
I am no longer among
The wolves
In the den.
I am home,
Comfortable by the fire.

Was it just a dream?

Three years...
I still dream of
The encounter
with the wolf.
Each day, I look out
From my window;
I see the crystal eyes,
Gazing back at me.

My hope:
The wolf and I
Will meet again
Someday soon.

www.ingramcontent.com/pod-product-compliance
Lightning Source LLC
Chambersburg PA
CBHW032047090426
42744CB00004B/110